The Girl Who Found God in an Orange

Dana Howard

Taste and see that the Lord is good; blessed is the one who takes refuge in Him.

Psalm 34:8

DEDICATION

For the girl who is tired. For the girl who is healing. For the girl who is trying. For the girl who feels too much and carries more than she ever says. For the girl who hopes for more than she knows how to put into words.

This is for you.

May you find God in the places you least expect Him. May you taste His sweetness in the middle of your storms. May you discover that He has been holding you — every moment, every breath, every chapter — all along.

ACKNOWLEDGMENTS

To the One who whispered this book into my heart — every word belongs to You.

To the women who have sat with me in the hard seasons, who have prayed for me, who have believed in me when I could barely breathe — your love is woven into every chapter.

To the readers who carry tenderness in their bones and hope in their hands — thank you for letting my story touch yours.

And to the girl I used to be — thank you for surviving long enough to become the woman who could write this.

How This Book Found Me

I didn't set out to write a book about an orange. I set out to survive a season that felt too heavy for my own strength.

There was a moment — in a hospital room where everything felt uncertain — when someone handed me an orange. I didn't know then how much I needed something simple to hold. Something bright. Something whole. Something that reminded me I was still here.

I didn't understand it at the time, but God was placing something in my hands long before I knew it was Him.

Later, in the quiet, in exhaustion, in prayer, I began to notice the way He kept showing up in that same small, ordinary thing. In the color. In the fragrance. In the sweetness. In the seeds. In the strength. In the segments. In the hands that held it. In the orchard it came from.

This book is not about fruit. It's about a God who hides Himself in the ordinary so we can find Him when we feel lost.

It's about a girl who discovered that healing doesn't always come in dramatic moments — sometimes it comes in small, bright, unexpected ways.

And it's about you — because somewhere in these pages, I believe you will find a piece of your own story.

TABLE OF CONTENTS

Part One — The Encounter

Part Two — The Inner Work

Part Three — The Surrender

PART ONE

The Encounter

CHAPTER 1

The Day the Orange Found Me

*The Lord is close to the brokenhearted and saves those
who are crushed in spirit.*
Psalm 34:18

A girl's reflection:

I didn't expect anything from God that morning. My heart felt
tired — the kind of tired that sits deep and doesn't move. Life
had been heavy for too long, and I didn't have the strength to
pretend otherwise.

I sat at my kitchen table with an orange in my hand. I wasn't
looking for meaning. I wasn't trying to be spiritual. I just
needed something simple to hold.

When I pressed my thumb into the peel, the fragrance filled
the air — bright and warm, almost like it had been waiting for
me.

And in that moment, something inside me stirred. Not a loud
voice. Not a dramatic revelation. Just a gentle awareness:

"I am here."

I didn't hear it with my ears. I felt it in the quiet place inside
me — the place where God whispers when I'm too weary to
listen any other way.

The orange suddenly felt like more than fruit. It felt like a reminder. A small, unexpected touch from a God who knew exactly how fragile I was.

The color. The fragrance. The sweetness. The way it opened in my hands.

It all felt like Him — gentle, patient, near.

And for the first time in a long time, I breathed a little deeper. God wasn't far away. He wasn't waiting for me to be stronger. He wasn't disappointed in my weakness.

He was simply… near.

I didn't know then that this moment would become a doorway — a way He would speak to me again and again through something so small.

But He did. And it began with an orange.

From the One who knows her:

My daughter, I came to you gently because I knew how tired you were. I knew the weight you carried. I knew the ache you didn't have words for.

So I met you in a way your heart could receive — not in thunder, not in fire, but in something simple enough to rest in your hands.

I have always spoken to you like this. Quietly. Tenderly. Through the moments you overlook. Through the ordinary things that carry My presence.

You didn't find Me in the orange. I found you.

And I will keep finding you — in small ways, in soft ways, in ways that remind you that I am not finished with you. I never will be.

A Gentle Prayer

Lord, open my heart to notice You in the simple places. Meet me in the moments I overlook. Lift the heaviness from my spirit and breathe Your nearness into the room. Thank You for coming close when I feel worn and fragile. Thank You for finding me. Amen.

.

CHAPTER 2

The Peel: God's Protection in Every Storm

I will give you a new heart and put a new
spirit in you.
Ezekiel 36:26

A girl's reflection:

There are parts of my story I used to avoid — not because I forgot them, but because I remembered them too clearly. Some memories felt sharp. Some felt heavy. Some felt too tangled to touch without reopening wounds I had worked hard to close.

But God doesn't peel back our layers harshly. He doesn't force healing. He doesn't rush the process. He meets us gently, right where our hearts can bear it.

When I think about the peel of an orange, I think about protection — the kind that surrounds you even when you don't know you're being held together.

For a long time, I didn't see God's protection in my story. I thought I survived because I was stubborn, or strong, or too used to pain to fall apart completely.

But now, when I look back, I see the peel.

I see it in the nights I cried myself to sleep and somehow woke up with enough strength to keep going. I see it in the moments that should have destroyed me but didn't. I see it in the car flipping on the drive home from California — metal twisting, glass breaking — and yet I crawled out alive. I see it in the seasons when I had nowhere to go and no one to lean on. I see it in the people God sent at the exact moment I needed them — the friend who stayed beside me in the storm; Robyn, who encouraged me to write; strangers who became lifelines.

The peel was there the whole time. Even when I felt forgotten. Even when I felt unprotected. Even when I thought God wasn't paying attention.

His protection didn't stop the storms. But it kept the storms from taking me out.

And that's what I didn't understand until much later:

God's protection doesn't always look like prevention. Sometimes it looks like survival. Sometimes it looks like breath in your lungs when you thought you were done. Sometimes it looks like a door closing that you begged Him to keep open. Sometimes it looks like a storm that should have killed you but didn't.

The peel is the reason I'm still here. The reason I can tell this story. The reason I can see God's hand in places I once avoided.

He protected me long before I knew how to see it.

From the One who knows her:

My daughter, you have never walked a single step without My covering.

You saw storms. I saw you wrapped in My hands.

You saw danger. I saw the boundaries I placed around you.

You saw the car flip. I saw the angels holding you steady.

You saw loneliness. I saw the seeds I was planting in the quiet.

You saw abandonment. I saw the moment you would learn that I never left.

You thought you were surviving on your own. But every breath you took was under My protection. Every tear you cried was caught by Me. Every moment you endured was held within My care.

You didn't recognize My covering because it didn't look the way you expected. You wanted Me to stop the storm. But I chose to carry you through it.

Nothing touched you without passing through My hands first. Nothing broke you beyond what I could heal. Nothing stole from you what I could not restore.

You are here because I covered you. You are whole because I held you. You are alive because My protection never failed — and it never will.

A Gentle Prayer

Lord, thank You for the protection I didn't see. Thank You for covering me in every storm, even when I felt alone. Peel back the layers of fear and help me trust Your care more deeply. Teach me to recognize Your protection in the moments that don't make sense. Hold me close, and keep me safe in Your hands. Amen.

CHAPTER 3

The Color: Warmth in the Cold Seasons

Arise, shine, for your light has come.
Isaiah 60:1

A girl's reflection:

There are seasons that don't feel dark — just dull. Not dramatic. Not overwhelming. Just… muted. Like the color has drained out of everything and you're moving through your days on autopilot.

I've lived through seasons like that. Times when I woke up and felt nothing. Times when I kept going because stopping felt harder. Times when joy felt like a language I used to speak but couldn't remember anymore.

In those moments, I didn't need something big from God. I didn't need a miracle or a sign in the sky. I just needed warmth — something small enough for my tired heart to hold.

That's what the color orange became for me.

It wasn't just a color. It was a reminder that warmth still existed. A soft glow in the cold places of my life. A whisper that God hadn't left me numb or forgotten.

Orange is the color of sunrise after a long night. The color of hope returning slowly. The color of breath coming back into lungs that forgot how to expand. The color of God saying, "I'm still here."

When I held that orange in my hand, I didn't just see fruit. I saw warmth. I saw light. I saw the promise that cold seasons don't last forever.

God doesn't always show up as fire. Sometimes He shows up as warmth — not enough to blind you, just enough to thaw you.

There were days when I felt frozen inside — frozen by fear, by exhaustion, by disappointment, by the weight of trying to be strong for too long.

But God kept slipping warmth into my life in ways I didn't recognize at the time:

A kind word. A moment of laughter. A sunrise I didn't expect to notice. A memory that softened instead of stinging. A breath that felt easier than the one before.

Little pockets of orange. Little reminders that I wasn't as alone as I felt.

The color of an orange doesn't shout. It glows. And that's how God met me in my cold seasons — not with pressure, not with noise, but with warmth.

From the One who knows her:

My beloved, I never asked you to pretend you weren't cold.

I saw the seasons when your heart felt numb. I saw the mornings when getting out of bed felt impossible. I saw the days when you smiled on the outside but felt empty inside.

I was not disappointed in you. I was not waiting for you to "snap out of it." I was sitting with you in the cold.

I wrapped My presence around you like a blanket. I placed small lights along your path — moments of warmth you didn't always notice. I whispered hope into the quiet places of your soul.

You thought you were fading. But I was coloring you back to life.

I didn't rush your healing. I didn't force your joy. I didn't demand your strength.

I simply stayed.

I warmed you slowly, gently, faithfully — the way the sun rises without effort, without noise, without hurry.

You don't have to fear the cold seasons. I am the warmth that returns every time. I am the color that breaks through the gray. I am the light that never leaves. And even when you cannot feel Me, I am still glowing over you.

A Gentle Prayer

Lord, thank You for being my warmth in the cold seasons. Thank You for coloring my life with hope when everything feels gray. Help me notice the small moments of light You place along my path. Wrap me in Your presence, and let Your gentle warmth thaw the places that feel frozen. Amen.

CHAPTER 4

The Fragrance: When God Walks into the Room

For we are to God the pleasing aroma of Christ.
2 Corinthians 2:15

A girl's reflection:

There is something unmistakable about the moment an orange is opened. You don't have to see it. You don't have to touch it. You don't even have to be close.

You just know.

The fragrance fills the room instantly — bright, sweet, alive. It spreads without effort. It lingers long after the fruit is gone.

That's what God's presence has always been like for me.

Not loud. Not forceful. Not dramatic.

Just unmistakable.

There were moments in my life when I didn't know how to pray. Moments when I didn't have the strength to open my Bible. Moments when I couldn't form words or pretend to be okay.

But then — something shifted. Something softened. Something breathed into the room.

A warmth. A stillness. A quiet awareness that I wasn't alone.

I didn't always recognize it as God. Sometimes I thought it was just a moment of peace. Sometimes I thought it was my mind finally calming down. Sometimes I thought it was coincidence.

But now I know better.

It was Him. It was always Him.

The fragrance of His presence has followed me through every chapter of my life — even the ones I tried to forget. Even the ones I didn't want to talk about. Even the ones where I felt too tired, too ashamed, too overwhelmed.

God doesn't wait for us to be ready. He doesn't wait for us to be strong. He doesn't wait for us to be spiritual enough or healed enough.

He just walks into the room.

Sometimes His presence feels like a sudden wave of peace. Sometimes it feels like a memory that warms instead of wounds. Sometimes it feels like a breath you didn't realize you were holding finally releasing.

Sometimes it feels like nothing at all — until later, when you look back and realize you were carried.

The fragrance of God is not something you earn. It's something you receive.

It's the reminder that He is near — closer than your breath, closer than your thoughts, closer than your pain.

And like the scent of an orange, His presence lingers. Even after the moment passes. Even after the prayer ends. Even after the tears dry.

He stays.

From the One who knows her:

My daughter, My presence has never depended on your strength.

You have felt Me in ways you didn't recognize — in the quiet, in the stillness, in the moments when you thought you were alone.

I walked into rooms you cried in. I sat beside you in the places you tried to hide. I breathed peace into the air when your heart was trembling.

I wrapped you in My presence when you didn't know how to reach for Me.

You thought you were failing. But you were simply exhausted. And I was not disappointed in you.

I do not enter your life with noise. I do not demand your attention. I do not force you to notice Me.

I come like fragrance — gentle, unmistakable, surrounding you without pressure.

You don't have to strive to feel Me. You don't have to earn My nearness. You don't have to perform for My presence.

I am already here. I have always been here. In every room. In every season. In every breath.

And when you open your heart — even a little — My presence fills the space instantly.

Just like the fragrance of an orange.

A Gentle Prayer

Lord, thank You for the gentle ways You enter my life. Thank You for filling the room with Your presence even when I don't have the words to pray. Teach me to recognize the fragrance of Your nearness. Let Your peace settle over my heart and linger long after the moment has passed. Amen.

PART TWO

The Inner Work

CHAPTER 5

The Sweetness: God's Kindness in Small Portions

Taste and see that the Lord is good.
Psalm 34:8

A girl's reflection:

There is a sweetness to an orange that feels honest. Not overwhelming. Not artificial. Not the kind of sweetness that leaves you aching afterward.

Just simple. Pure. Enough.

When I think about the sweetness of God, I think about the quiet moments when His kindness slipped into my life so gently I almost missed it.

Not the big miracles — though I've seen those too — but the small mercies that showed up like soft reminders that I was loved.

God's sweetness rarely arrives all at once. It comes in pieces. In moments. In breaths.

Just like an orange gives you one segment at a time.

There were seasons when I begged God for breakthrough, for clarity, for answers, for relief. I wanted Him to fix everything in a single moment. I wanted Him to sweep in and change my life all at once.

But instead, He gave me sweetness.

A text from a friend at the exact moment I felt forgotten. A laugh that rose up after days of heaviness. A sunrise painted in colors I didn't know I needed. A moment of peace in the middle of chaos. A breath that felt easier than the one before.

Small portions. Small mercies. Small sweetnesses.

At the time, I didn't always appreciate them. I wanted more. I wanted bigger. I wanted answers, not moments.

But now I see what I couldn't see then:

God was feeding me gently.

He knew my heart couldn't handle the whole fruit. He knew I was too tired, too overwhelmed, too stretched thin to receive everything I was asking for.

He knew I needed sweetness in small, manageable pieces.

Just enough for the day. Just enough for the moment. Just enough to keep going.

God's kindness is not loud. It's not dramatic. It's not rushed.

It's sweet. It's steady. And it's always enough.

From the One who knows her:

My daughter, I have never withheld goodness from you.

I have given you sweetness in every season — even the ones that felt bitter.

I placed small gifts along your path, knowing exactly what your heart could hold. I fed you gently — not because you were weak, but because you were healing.

You asked Me for answers. I gave you peace.

You asked Me for breakthrough. I gave you strength.

You asked Me for clarity. I gave you rest.

You asked Me for the whole story. I gave you one piece at a time.

Not to frustrate you. Not to delay you. Not to punish you.

But to protect you.

If I had given you everything at once, it would have overwhelmed you. If I had revealed the whole plan, it would have frightened you. If I had poured out all the sweetness at once, it would have been too much for your weary heart.

So I gave you portions. Segments. Moments.

Each one chosen with care. Each one timed with precision. Each one carrying exactly what you needed.

You have never gone a day without My kindness. You have never walked a mile without My sweetness. You have never faced a moment without My mercy.

Taste what I give you, daughter. It is enough for today.

And tomorrow, I will give you more.

A Gentle Prayer

Lord, thank You for the sweetness You place in my life, even when I don't recognize it. Teach me to notice the small mercies, the gentle gifts, the quiet kindnesses You give me each day. Help me trust the portions You provide, and rest in the truth that Your goodness is always enough. Amen.

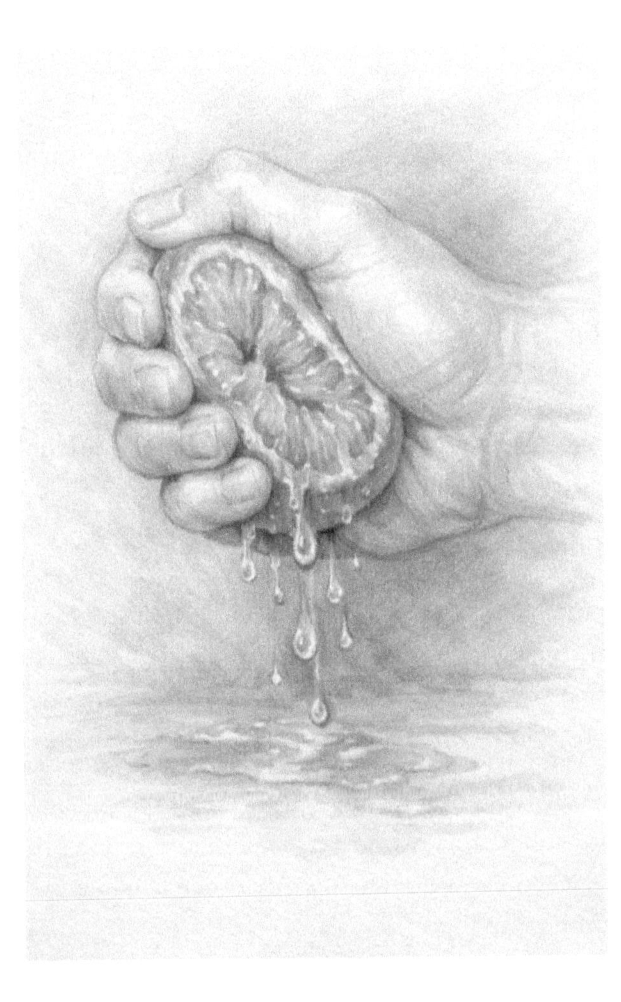

CHAPTER 6

The Juice: The Strength You Didn't Know You Had

*I can do all things through Christ
who strengthens me.*
Philippians 4:13

A girl's reflection:

There is something almost miraculous about the juice inside an orange. You don't see it from the outside. You don't hear it. You don't feel it until the fruit is opened.

But it's there — hidden, waiting, sustaining.

That's what God's strength has been like in my life. Quiet. Unseen. Steady. Flowing through me even when I didn't realize it.

There were seasons when I was running on empty — emotionally, physically, spiritually. Seasons when I was carrying more than any one person should ever have to carry. Seasons when I was holding up other people while trying not to collapse myself.

I didn't feel strong. I didn't look strong. I didn't believe I was strong.

But somehow, I kept going. Somehow, I kept showing up. Somehow, I kept breathing. Somehow, I kept surviving.

And now, looking back, I know why.

It wasn't my strength. It was His.

God's strength doesn't always feel like power. Sometimes it feels like endurance. Sometimes it feels like one more step. Sometimes it feels like not giving up today. Sometimes it feels like a breath you didn't think you could take.

The juice inside an orange is what keeps it alive. The strength inside you is what kept you alive.

There were days when I thought I had nothing left. Days when I felt drained, depleted, poured out. Days when I whispered, "I can't do this anymore," and yet somehow — I did.

That wasn't me. That was God.

His strength flowed through me drop by drop. Not in a flood. Not in a surge. Not in a dramatic burst of power.

But in quiet, steady, sustaining grace.

The kind of strength that doesn't announce itself. The kind that doesn't make you feel invincible. The kind that simply keeps you from falling apart.

The juice of an orange is hidden until pressure is applied. God's strength in me was the same.

It showed up under pressure. It revealed itself in the crushing. It flowed when life squeezed me.

And even when I felt empty, God kept refilling me — not all at once, but enough for the moment. Enough for the hour. Enough for the day. Enough to keep going.

From the One who knows her:

My daughter, the strength you felt was Mine.

You thought you were surviving on your own. You thought you were pushing through by sheer willpower. You thought you were holding everything together by yourself.

But every step you took was carried by Me. Every breath you drew was sustained by Me. Every moment you endured was strengthened by Me.

You didn't feel powerful — and that is exactly why My power could flow through you.

My strength is not loud. It is not forceful. It is not overwhelming.

It is steady. It is quiet. It is constant.

I gave you strength when you didn't ask for it. I poured endurance into you when you felt empty. I held you up when you were too tired to stand. I breathed life into you when you felt drained.

You didn't see the strength inside you because it wasn't yours — it was Mine.

And I will keep giving it to you. Not in overwhelming waves, but in steady streams. Not in dramatic moments, but in daily mercies. Not in sudden bursts, but in quiet endurance.

You will never run out of strength as long as you draw from Me. I am your source. I am your sustainer. I am the life flowing through you.

And I will never stop pouring.

A Gentle Prayer

Lord, thank You for being my strength when I feel empty. Thank You for sustaining me in ways I didn't recognize at the time. Teach me to draw from Your power instead of my own. Fill me with the quiet endurance I need for today, and remind me that Your strength never runs dry. Amen.

CHAPTER 7

The Seeds: Promises Buried Deep

*For at the proper time we will reap a harvest if we do not
give up.*
Galatians 6:9

A girl's reflection:

Seeds are strange things. They look small. Unimpressive. Easy
to overlook.

But inside every seed is a future waiting to unfold — a future
you can't see yet, a future that looks nothing like the shell it's
wrapped in.

When I think about the seeds inside an orange, I think about
the promises God planted in me long before I understood
what He was doing.

Some seeds were planted in childhood — moments of
tenderness, moments of sensitivity, moments where I felt
things deeply and didn't know why.

Some were planted in pain — seasons where everything
familiar fell apart, where I was stripped down to nothing,
where I had no choice but to cling to God even when I
couldn't feel Him.

Some were planted in silence — years where I didn't hear answers, didn't see progress, didn't understand the purpose.

Seeds don't grow the moment they're planted. They grow in darkness. They grow underground. They grow where no one can see.

And for a long time, I didn't see anything growing in me.

I saw survival. I saw exhaustion. I saw heartbreak. I saw disappointment. I saw waiting.

But I didn't see growth. I didn't see purpose. I didn't see promise.

I didn't see the seeds.

Not yet.

It wasn't until much later — when I started writing, when the words poured out of me like water breaking through a dam — that I realized something had been growing inside me all along.

The tenderness. The depth. The voice. The calling. The compassion. The ministry. The ability to speak to people's hearts in a way that felt like breath.

None of that appeared out of nowhere.

It was planted. Buried. Hidden. Growing in the dark.

The seeds God plants in us rarely look like what they will become. They rarely make sense at the time. They rarely feel significant.

But they are.

Every seed in your life carries a promise. Every promise carries a future. Every future carries fruit.

And God wastes nothing — not even the buried things.

From the One who knows her:

My daughter, I planted more in you than you know.

You saw pain. I saw preparation.

You saw loss. I saw planting.

You saw silence. I saw roots forming.

You saw delay. I saw timing.

Nothing in your life has been wasted. Not a single tear. Not a single season. Not a single moment of waiting.

I planted seeds in you long before you understood My voice — seeds of compassion, tenderness, wisdom, creativity, calling, and ministry.

You thought they were buried because you had failed. But they were buried because they were meant to grow.

Seeds grow in hidden places. They grow in the dark. They grow in the soil of surrender. They grow in the places where you feel forgotten.

But I never forgot you. I never left you. I never stopped tending the garden of your heart.

Every seed I planted in you is rising. Every promise I whispered is unfolding. Every dream you thought was dead is coming back to life.

You are not behind. You are not late. You are not overlooked.

You are blooming right on time.

A Gentle Prayer

Lord, thank You for the seeds You've planted in my life — the ones I see and the ones still hidden. Help me trust the seasons of waiting, the seasons of darkness, the seasons where nothing seems to be growing. Teach me to believe that every buried thing has purpose and that Your promises always rise. Amen.

The Segments: God Gives You What You Need When You Need It

Give us this day our daily bread.
Matthew 6:11

A girl's reflection:

An orange never gives you everything at once. It comes in segments — small, gentle pieces that fit right into your hand. You take it one piece at a time.

And that's exactly how God has always given me what I needed.

Not all at once. Not in overwhelming amounts. Not in a way that would drown me.

But in portions. In moments. In quiet, measured pieces of grace.

There were seasons when I begged God for the whole picture. I wanted clarity. I wanted certainty. I wanted to know how everything would turn out.

But God didn't give me the whole story.

He gave me a segment.

A moment of peace in the middle of fear. A small breakthrough after months of waiting. A single open door when everything else was closed. A whisper of hope when I felt like giving up.

Just enough to keep going. Just enough to take the next step. Just enough to trust Him for one more day.

At the time, I didn't understand it. I thought God was withholding. I thought He was delaying. I thought He was silent.

But now I see what I couldn't see then:

He was protecting me.

If God had given me everything I asked for all at once, it would have overwhelmed me. If He had revealed the whole journey, I would have run in the opposite direction. If He had answered every prayer immediately, I wouldn't have learned how to trust Him in the waiting.

God gives in segments because He knows what our hearts can hold.

He knows when we're ready for the next piece. He knows when we need to pause and breathe. He knows when we need rest more than answers.

And He knows that too much sweetness at once can make us sick.

So He gives us what we need when we need it. Not a moment too early. Not a moment too late.

Just right. Just enough. Just in time.

The segments of my life haven't always made sense on their own. Some were bitter. Some were sweet. Some were confusing. Some were healing.

But together, they form a story I never could have written on my own — a story of timing, a story of mercy, a story of a God who portions life with tenderness.

Piece by piece. Segment by segment. Grace by grace.

From the One who knows her:

My daughter, I have never withheld anything from you.

I have only given you what your heart was ready to receive.

You wanted the whole fruit. I gave you segments — not to frustrate you, but to protect you.

I know the weight you can carry. I know the pace your soul needs. I know the timing that will not break you.

I give you what you need for today — not because I am limited, but because I am wise.

If I gave you everything at once, you would rush ahead without Me. You would try to run on tomorrow's strength instead of today's grace. You would be overwhelmed by blessings you weren't ready to hold.

So I portion My goodness in pieces.

I give you peace for this moment. Strength for this hour. Mercy for this day. Hope for this season.

And when you need more, I will give you more.

You will never run out of what you need as long as you stay close to Me.

I am not withholding. I am providing. I am not delaying. I am preparing. I am not silent. I am speaking in portions your heart can receive.

Trust the timing, beloved. Trust the segments. Trust the way I feed your soul.

I am giving you exactly what you need — exactly when you need it.

A Gentle Prayer

Lord, thank You for giving me what my heart can hold. Teach me to trust Your timing, Your portions, Your wisdom. Help me receive the grace You offer today without rushing ahead or reaching back. Give me peace for this moment and faith for the next. Amen.

PART THREE

The Surrender

CHAPTER 9

The Hands That Hold The Fruit: Surrendering What Was Never Yours To Carry

I will uphold you with My righteous right hand.
Isaiah 41:10

A girl's reflection:

There is a moment when you hold an orange in your hands and realize something simple but true:

You are not the source of anything inside it.

You didn't grow the tree. You didn't form the fruit. You didn't create the sweetness, the fragrance, the color, the seeds, or the strength within it.

All you did was receive it.

And yet for so much of my life, I lived as if everything depended on me.

I carried burdens that were never mine. I held responsibilities that were too heavy. I tried to fix things I didn't have the power to fix. I tried to hold people together while I was falling apart myself.

I thought surrender meant failure. I thought letting go meant giving up. I thought releasing control meant I wasn't strong enough.

But the truth is, I was never meant to carry the weight I was holding.

There were seasons when my hands were full — full of fear, full of worry, full of expectations, full of pressure, full of things I thought I had to manage on my own.

And God kept whispering, "Give it to Me."

But I didn't know how. I didn't know what surrender looked like. I didn't know how to trust hands I couldn't see.

Until one day, I realized something:

The same God who created the fruit knows how to hold it. And the same God who created me knows how to hold my life.

Surrender isn't dropping everything in defeat. It's placing everything into stronger hands.

It's saying, "I can't carry this anymore," and hearing God respond, "You were never meant to."

It's opening your fingers one by one and letting God take what has been crushing you.

It's trusting that His hands are steady. Gentle. Sure. Capable.

It's believing that you don't have to be the strong one all the time. You don't have to hold every piece of your life together. You don't have to grip what is slipping away. You don't have to manage what is too heavy. You don't have to carry what breaks you.

Your hands were made to receive. His hands were made to hold.

From the One who knows her:

My daughter, you were never meant to carry the weight you've been holding.

I did not design your hands to grip fear. I did not shape your fingers to cling to burdens. I did not form your heart to live in constant strain.

Your hands were made to open. To receive. To release.

Mine were made to hold.

You have tried so hard to be strong. To manage everything. To protect yourself. To protect others. To keep your world from falling apart.

But beloved, that is My job.

Let Me carry what is too heavy for you. Let Me hold what you cannot fix. Let Me take what has been weighing you down.

You do not disappoint Me when you surrender. You honor Me.

Because surrender is not weakness — it is trust.

Place your fears in My hands. Place your future in My hands. Place your people, your dreams, your wounds, your questions in My hands.

I will not drop what you give Me. I will not mishandle what you release. I will not lose what you entrust to Me.

My hands are steady. My hands are gentle. My hands are strong.

And they are holding you even now.

A Gentle Prayer

Lord, I place into Your hands what I can no longer carry. Take the weight, the fear, the pressure, the expectations, and the burdens that have been crushing me. Teach me to trust Your steady hands more than my own. Help me release what was never mine to hold. Amen.

CHAPTER 10

The Fruit Itself: A Life That Reflects The One Who Made It

*If you remain in Me and I in you, you will
bear much fruit.*
John 15:5

A girl's reflection:

When you hold an orange in your hands, you're holding more than fruit. You're holding a story.

A story of sunlight and rain. A story of roots and soil. A story of quiet growth that happened long before you ever touched it.

And in a way, that's what my life has become — a story shaped by a God who was working long before I understood what He was doing.

The fruit is the visible part. The part you can taste and see. The part that looks whole.

But it's also the part that took the longest to form.

For so much of my life, I didn't feel like fruit. I felt like fragments. Pieces. Segments. Seeds. Peel. Juice. Color. Fragrance.

Parts of me made sense. Parts of me didn't. Parts of me felt sweet. Parts of me felt bitter. Parts of me felt hidden. Parts of me felt broken.

But slowly — gently — God began gathering every part of me into something whole.

He took the sweetness and the strength. He took the seeds and the segments. He took the color and the fragrance. He took the peel that protected me and the juice that sustained me.

And He formed something I never expected:

A life that reflects Him.

Not perfectly. Not without scars. Not without questions or seasons of silence.

But honestly. Tenderly. Beautifully.

The fruit of my life is not my achievement. It is His work.

It is the evidence of a God who stayed through every season. A God who protected me when I didn't know I needed protection. A God who warmed me when I felt cold inside. A God who strengthened me when I was empty. A God who planted promises in the dark and brought them to life in His time.

The fruit of my life is not about perfection. It's about presence.

His presence in every chapter. His presence in every storm. His presence in every breath.

And now, when people taste the fruit of who I've become —
the tenderness, the compassion, the depth, the voice, the
ministry — I hope they taste Him.

Because everything good in me came from Him. Everything
sweet. Everything strong. Everything healing. Everything
hopeful.

The fruit of my life is simply the evidence that God never left.

From the One who knows her:

My daughter, you are the fruit of My faithfulness.

*You are the evidence of My nearness. You are the reflection
of My tenderness. You are the living proof that I stay
through every season.*

*I shaped you with intention. I formed you with care. I
tended you with patience. I watered you with mercy. I
warmed you with My presence.*

*Nothing in your life was wasted. Nothing was random.
Nothing was overlooked.*

*Every season served a purpose. Every tear watered
something. Every waiting period rooted something. Every
storm strengthened something.*

And now, the fruit of your life is ripening.

Not because you tried harder. Not because you earned it. Not because you were strong enough.

But because I was faithful.

The sweetness you carry is Mine. The strength you carry is Mine. The compassion you offer is Mine. The hope you speak is Mine.

You are not the source of the fruit. You are the vessel.

And I will continue to grow beauty in you — season after season, year after year, moment by moment.

Your life is My garden. Your heart is My home. Your story is My glory.

And I delight in the fruit you bear.

A Gentle Prayer

Lord, thank You for shaping my life with such tenderness. Thank You for gathering every part of me into something whole. Teach me to reflect Your sweetness, Your strength, Your compassion, and Your presence in everything I do. Let the fruit of my life point back to You in every season. Amen.

CHAPTER 11

The Sharing: When Your Story Becomes Someone Elses's Nourishment

He comforts us... so that we can comfort those
in any trouble.
2 Corinthians 1:4

A girl's reflection:

There is something tender about offering someone a piece of your orange. It's small. Simple. Ordinary.

But it's also intimate — a quiet way of saying, "Here… take what helped me."

I didn't always believe my story could feed anyone. For a long time, I thought my life was too messy, too complicated, too broken to offer anything to anyone else.

I thought healing had to be complete before it could be shared. I thought testimonies had to be polished before they could be spoken. I thought fruit had to be perfect before it could be given.

But God kept whispering, "Give them what you have."

Not the whole fruit. Not the whole story. Not the whole journey.

Just a piece.

A moment of honesty. A sentence of hope. A breath of truth. A glimpse of what God has done in me.

And every time I shared even a small piece of my story, something happened.

Someone breathed easier. Someone felt seen. Someone felt less alone. Someone whispered, "I needed that."

I didn't realize that the sweetness God placed in my life was never meant to stay with me.

Fruit is meant to be shared.

Your healing feeds someone else's hope. Your survival feeds someone else's strength. Your honesty feeds someone else's courage. Your tenderness feeds someone else's heart.

And your story — the one you thought was too messy, too painful, too complicated — becomes nourishment for someone who is starving for reassurance that God is still near.

I used to think I had to be whole before I could help anyone.

But now I know:

God uses broken fruit too.

He uses the pieces. He uses the segments. He uses the parts that feel unfinished.

Because what nourishes people is not perfection — it's presence. It's honesty. It's the sweetness of a life touched by God.

And when you share even a small piece of what He's done in you, you become part of someone else's healing.

From the One who knows her:

My daughter, your story is not just for you.

The sweetness I placed in you was meant to be tasted by others. The strength I poured into you was meant to steady someone else. The healing I brought you through was meant to become a doorway for another heart.

You do not need to be perfect to be used. You do not need to be finished to be fruitful. You do not need to be whole to be a blessing.

I use the pieces. I use the cracks. I use the places you thought disqualified you.

When you share your story, you are not giving people your strength — you are giving them Mine.

You are offering a taste of My goodness, a glimpse of My faithfulness, a whisper of My presence.

Do not hide what I have done in you. Do not shrink back from the sweetness I've placed in your hands. Do not underestimate the power of a single segment offered in love.

Your story is nourishment. Your voice is medicine. Your honesty is healing.

And I will use you to feed many.

A Gentle Prayer

Lord, thank You for the sweetness You've placed in my life. Teach me to share it with courage and tenderness. Use my story to nourish others, to comfort them, to remind them that You are near. Let my life be a small offering that points back to Your goodness. Amen..

CHAPTER 12

The Leftovers: Nothing In God's Hands Is Wasted

*Gather the pieces that are left over. Let nothing
be wasted.*
John 6:12

A girl's reflection:

When you finish eating an orange, there are always pieces left
behind. Bits of peel. A few threads of pith. Seeds you didn't
need. Drops of juice on your fingers. Fragments that seem too
small to matter.

Most people throw them away without a second thought.

But God doesn't.

God has never looked at the leftovers of my life and seen
waste.

He has never looked at the pieces I thought were useless —
the broken moments, the painful memories, the seasons I
regretted, the mistakes I made, the years I felt lost — and
dismissed them as meaningless.

I did. But He didn't.

There were parts of my story I wanted to forget. Parts I wished had never happened. Parts I thought disqualified me from being used by God.

But slowly, gently, patiently, He began to show me that the pieces I wanted to throw away were the very pieces He wanted to redeem.

The tears I cried watered compassion. The loneliness I felt made room for tenderness. The storms I survived built endurance. The heartbreak I carried taught me how to love deeply. The mistakes I made became wisdom. The seasons I thought were wasted became soil for something new.

God doesn't waste anything.

Not the years you spent trying to heal. Not the nights you spent crying alone. Not the prayers you whispered with trembling hands. Not the moments you felt like you were failing. Not the chapters you wish you could rewrite.

He gathers every leftover with care.

He holds the pieces you think are too small to matter. He collects the fragments you think are too broken to be used. He saves the moments you think are too painful to redeem.

And He turns them into something beautiful.

The leftovers of my life are not trash. They are testimony.

They are the proof that God can take what I thought was ruined and turn it into something that feeds others. They are the evidence that nothing in His hands is ever wasted.

From the One who knows her:

My daughter, I have never thrown away a single piece of your story.

Not the broken pieces. Not the painful pieces. Not the confusing pieces. Not the pieces you tried to hide. Not the pieces you thought were failures.

I have gathered them all.

Every tear you cried is stored with Me. Every prayer you whispered is held by Me. Every moment you survived is remembered by Me.

You see leftovers. I see ingredients. You see waste. I see purpose. You see fragments. I see a future.

Nothing in your life has been meaningless. Nothing has been random. Nothing has been beyond My ability to redeem.

I use the pieces you want to forget. I use the moments you regret. I use the seasons you thought were lost.

I weave them into something beautiful — a story that carries My fingerprints, My faithfulness, My redemption.

You are not defined by what you lost. You are defined by what I can restore.

And I will restore everything.

Nothing in My hands is ever wasted.

A Gentle Prayer

Lord, thank You for gathering the pieces of my life with such tenderness. Help me trust that nothing in my story is beyond Your redemption. Teach me to release the moments I regret and believe that You can use even the leftovers for something beautiful. Make my life a testimony of Your restoring love. Amen.

PART FOUR

The Becoming

CHAPTER 13

The Table: Where God Feeds You And Invites You To Rest

You prepare a table before me.
Psalm 23:5

A girl's reflection:

There is something sacred about a table. A place to sit. A place to breathe. A place to receive instead of perform. A place where nourishment meets need without judgment.

For so much of my life, I didn't know how to sit at God's table.

I stood at the edges. I hovered near the doorway. I stayed busy, distracted, overwhelmed — trying to earn a seat that was already mine.

I thought I had to be better before I could come. I thought I had to be healed before I could sit. I thought I had to be whole before I could rest.

But God kept pulling out a chair and whispering, "Come sit with Me."

Not when I was strong. Not when I was steady. Not when I had everything figured out.

But now. As I was. As I am.

The table of God is not a place for the polished. It's a place for the tired. The hungry. The hurting. The ones who have been carrying too much for too long.

It's a place where striving ends and receiving begins.

When I picture God's table, I see an orange sitting there — bright, simple, whole.

A reminder that everything I need is already provided. A reminder that nourishment comes from His hands, not mine. A reminder that I don't have to earn what He freely gives.

At His table, I don't have to pretend. I don't have to perform. I don't have to hide the parts of me that feel unfinished.

I can just be.

And He meets me there with gentleness. With warmth. With sweetness. With strength. With truth. With rest.

The table of God is not a place of pressure. It's a place of presence.

A place where He feeds me what my soul is starving for. A place where He reminds me that I am safe. A place where He whispers, "You don't have to carry this alone."

A place where I finally learn to breathe again.

From the One who knows her:

My daughter, I prepared a place for you long before you knew you needed it.

A place to rest. A place to be held. A place to be nourished. A place to be known.

You do not have to earn your seat at My table. It is yours because you are Mine.

Come sit with Me when you are weary. Come sit with Me when you are overwhelmed. Come sit with Me when you feel unworthy. Come sit with Me when you don't know what you need.

I will feed you with peace. I will nourish you with hope. I will strengthen you with My presence. I will comfort you with My nearness.

You do not have to bring anything with you. You do not have to pretend to be strong. You do not have to hide your wounds.

Just come.

I will fill what is empty. I will calm what is anxious. I will heal what is hurting. I will carry what is heavy.

My table is a place of rest. A place of renewal. A place of belonging.

And there will always be a seat for you.

A Gentle Prayer

Lord, thank You for preparing a place where I can rest. Teach me to sit at Your table without fear, without striving, without pretending. Feed my soul with Your peace, Your presence, Your tenderness. Help me receive what You offer with open hands and a quiet heart. Amen.

CHAPTER 14

The Aftertaste: When God's Presence Lingers Long After The Moment Has Passed

In Your presence there is fullness of joy.
Psalm 16:11

A girl's reflection:

There's something almost surprising about the aftertaste of an orange. It stays with you — soft, sweet, bright — long after the fruit is gone. It lingers in a way you don't expect. Not loud. Not overwhelming. Just quietly present.

And that's exactly how God's presence has always felt in my life.

Not a momentary flash. Not a brief encounter. Not a single experience that fades with time.

But something that stays. Something that settles. Something that follows me into the hours and days and seasons that come after.

There were moments when I felt God so clearly — in the fragrance, in the sweetness, in the warmth, in the strength, in the quiet whisper that filled the room.

But what surprised me most wasn't the moment itself. It was the aftertaste.

The peace that lingered after the tears dried. The hope that stayed after the prayer ended. The clarity that remained after the confusion lifted. The comfort that held me long after the moment had passed.

God's presence doesn't evaporate when the feeling fades.

It settles into the deeper places — where memory meets faith, where experience meets trust, where encounter becomes transformation.

The aftertaste of God is the quiet knowing that you are not alone. The gentle awareness that He is still near. The soft reminder that He is not going anywhere.

Even when life gets loud. Even when fear returns. Even when the world pulls at your attention. Even when you forget the moment that changed you.

He doesn't forget.

His presence lingers like sweetness on the tongue — subtle, steady, comforting, real.

And sometimes, it's the aftertaste that carries you through the next season.

From the One who knows her:

My daughter, I do not visit you and then leave.

When I come close, I stay close. When I speak, My words remain. When I comfort you, My peace settles deep into your spirit.

You may not always feel Me with the same intensity, but I am never far.

My presence lingers in your thoughts, in your breath, in your memories, in the quiet places of your heart.

I am with you in the moments that feel holy and in the moments that feel ordinary.

I am with you in the sweetness and in the silence. In the clarity and in the questions. In the warmth and in the waiting.

You do not have to chase Me. You do not have to earn My nearness. You do not have to fear that I will disappear.

I remain. I stay. I linger.

And even when you move on to the next chapter of your life, I am already there — waiting, holding, guiding, loving.

My presence is the aftertaste your soul was made for.

A Gentle Prayer

Lord, thank You for the way Your presence lingers long after the moment has passed. Help me notice the quiet sweetness You leave behind. Let Your peace settle deep within me, and let the memory of Your nearness carry me into every season ahead. Amen..

CHAPTER 15

The Rind: What You Leave Behind When God Makes You New

The old has gone, the new is here.
2 Corinthians 5:17

A girl's reflection:

When you peel an orange, you don't keep the rind. You don't frame it. You don't treasure it. You don't carry it around like it's precious.

You let it go.

Because the rind is not the fruit. It's what had to come off so the fruit could be revealed.

There are parts of my life that were never meant to stay with me forever.

Old fears. Old identities. Old wounds. Old versions of myself I clung to because they felt familiar — even when they were hurting me.

There were seasons when I wrapped myself in layers of protection — walls I built, roles I played, masks I wore, stories I believed about who I was and who I wasn't.

Some of those layers kept me safe for a time. Some helped me survive. Some were necessary in the moment.

But they were never meant to define me.

They were rind — temporary coverings for a heart still growing.

And when God began peeling those layers away, I didn't understand what He was doing.

It felt like loss. It felt like exposure. It felt like being stripped of everything familiar.

But now I see what I couldn't see then:

He wasn't taking from me. He was revealing me.

He was removing what no longer served me. He was peeling away the lies I believed. He was stripping off the shame I carried. He was loosening the fear that held me. He was breaking open the hardness around my heart.

He was making room for the fruit.

The rind of my life was never meant to be permanent. It was meant to fall away.

And the moment I stopped trying to hold onto it — the moment I let God peel back what I no longer needed — I discovered something beautiful:

There was sweetness underneath I didn't know was there.

A tenderness. A strength. A voice. A calling. A softness. A courage. A newness I didn't recognize at first because I had lived so long wrapped in the old.

Letting go is not losing. It's becoming.

From the One who knows her:

My daughter, I never peel away anything without purpose.

Every layer I remove is something that once protected you but no longer serves you.

I peel away fear so you can walk in freedom. I peel away shame so you can stand in truth. I peel away old identities so you can embrace who you really are. I peel away heaviness so you can breathe again.

You are not losing yourself when I peel away the rind. You are finding yourself.

The girl you were helped you survive. The woman you are becoming will help others live.

Do not cling to what I am removing. Do not mourn what was never meant to stay. Do not fear the newness I am revealing.

You are not being stripped. You are being uncovered. You are not being diminished. You are being restored. You are not being broken. You are being made whole.

Let the rind fall away, beloved. There is fruit beneath it that the world needs to taste.

A Gentle Prayer

Lord, peel away the layers that no longer belong to me. Remove the fear, the shame, the old identities, and the heaviness I've carried. Reveal the sweetness You've placed beneath the surface. Make me new in the places I've grown used to being old. Amen.

CHAPTER 16

The Orchard: You Were Never Just One Fruit

This is to My Father's glory, that you bear much fruit.
John 15:8

A girl's reflection:

There is a moment when you step back from a single orange and realize it came from a tree. And that tree came from a seed. And that seed came from another fruit. And that fruit came from another tree.

And suddenly, you're not looking at one orange anymore. You're looking at an orchard.

A whole landscape of life and growth and seasons and stories that stretch far beyond what your eyes can see.

For so long, I thought my life was small. Just one story. Just one girl. Just one journey trying to make sense of God and pain and hope and healing.

But now I see what I couldn't see before:

My life is part of something bigger.

Every moment God healed me became a seed for someone else. Every word He gave me became nourishment for another heart. Every chapter of my story became a branch someone else could rest beneath.

I was never just one fruit. I was part of an orchard God has been growing for generations.

The people who poured into me — their tenderness, their encouragement, their prayers, their presence — they were trees that shaded me when I was weary.

And now, without even realizing it, I have become a tree too.

Not because I'm strong. Not because I'm perfect. Not because I have everything figured out.

But because God planted me with purpose. He watered me with mercy. He tended me with patience. He grew me through storms and seasons and sunlight and silence.

And now, the fruit of my life is not just for me.

It's for the ones who will come after. The ones who need shade. The ones who need sweetness. The ones who need hope. The ones who need a place to rest and breathe and remember that God is still good.

The orchard of God is made of stories like mine and stories like yours — ordinary lives that become extraordinary when touched by His hands.

And the most beautiful part?

The orchard is still growing.

From the One who knows her:

My daughter, you were never meant to stand alone.

I planted you in a story far bigger than your own. You are part of My orchard — a living, growing, ever-expanding testimony of My faithfulness.

The fruit of your life will nourish many. The shade of your branches will comfort the weary. The seeds you scatter through your words, your tenderness, your obedience, your healing — they will take root in places you may never see.

You are not responsible for the whole orchard. You are responsible for being faithful where I planted you.

And I will use you to grow beauty in the lives of others.

You are not small. You are not insignificant. You are not alone.

You are part of My great story — a story that began long before you and will continue long after you.

And every part of your life, every season, every chapter, every breath has been woven into something eternal.

You are My planting. You are My delight. You are My orchard in bloom.

A Gentle Prayer

Lord, thank You for planting my life in something bigger than I can see. Help me trust that my story matters, that my fruit has purpose, and that the seeds You've grown in me will bless others. Let my life be part of Your orchard — a place of shade, sweetness, and hope for every heart You bring my way. Amen.

EPILOGUE

When The Story Becomes Yours

There comes a moment when the girl sets the orange down and realizes the story was never just about her.

It was about you.

Your seasons. Your storms. Your sweetness. Your seeds. Your strength. Your healing. Your becoming.

The orange was simply a mirror — a way for you to see what God has been doing in your own life all along.

Every chapter you read was an invitation to notice Him again. To feel Him again. To trust Him again. To breathe again.

And now, as you close this book, you are not closing the story.

You are stepping into it.

You are the girl (or the woman, or the weary soul) who finds God in the ordinary. In the small. In the quiet. In the overlooked. In the simple sweetness of a moment you might have missed.

You are the one He has been tending. You are the one He has been healing. You are the one He has been shaping with tenderness.

And your life — your whole, beautiful, messy, holy life — is fruit in His hands.

This is not the end.

This is the beginning of seeing Him everywhere.

Even in an orange.

CLOSING BLESSING

May you feel God in the small things. May you find Him in the quiet places. May His warmth reach the cold corners of your heart. May His sweetness meet you gently. May His strength rise within you when you feel empty. May His promises grow in the dark until they bloom in the light. May His presence linger long after the moment has passed. And may your life become fruit — sweet, steady, nourishing — for every heart that needs hope.

FINAL PRAYER

For The One Who Reads This Book

Lord, for the one holding this book, I ask for tenderness. For warmth. For sweetness. For strength.

For healing in the places that feel hidden. For hope in the places that feel heavy. For light in the places that feel dim. For rest in the places that feel restless.

Meet her in the small moments — in the quiet breaths, in the ordinary places where she least expects You.

Let her feel Your nearness. Let her taste Your goodness. Let her see Your fingerprints on every chapter of her life.

And let her know — deep in her bones — that she is held, she is loved, she is seen, and she is never alone.

Amen.

ABOUT THE AUTHOR

Dana Howard writes for the tired, the tender, and the ones who feel everything deeply. Her words carry the quiet strength of someone who has walked through storms and found God not at the finish line, but in the middle of the mess. She writes from lived experience — from the valleys, not the mountaintops — offering comfort that feels personal, gentle, and real.

Dana is the author of Hope in Jesus: Comfort During the Storms of Life, a book born from seasons of pain where God met her with unexpected tenderness. Her writing is not theological or academic; it is intimate, breath-based, and rooted in the kind of hope that whispers rather than shouts.

She is also the founder of The Peace of Heaven, a ministry dedicated to offering daily encouragement to weary hearts. Her devotions, prayers, and reflections have reached readers around the world who long for a God who feels close, compassionate, and present in the ordinary moments of life.

Dana lives in Washington with her husband, John, and writes for those who need gentle hope. Her deepest desire is that every reader would feel seen, held, and loved by the God who walks with them through every chapter of their story.